I0605740

HISTORICAL AGES

THE STONE AGE

BY YVETTE LaPIERRE

An Imprint of Abdo Publishing
abdobooks.com

Cover image: In the later part of the Stone Age, some people began making pottery.

abdobooks.com

Published by Abdo Publishing, a division of ABDO, PO Box 398166, Minneapolis, Minnesota 55439.

Printed in the United States of America, North Mankato, Minnesota.
102024
012025

Cover Photo: Science History Images/Alamy
Interior Photos: Horst Ossinger/picture-alliance/dpa/AP Images, 4–5; Michael Latz/DDP/AFP/Getty Images, 7; Martin Meissner/AP Images, 8; Red Line Editorial, 10; Hugo Martin/Alamy, 12–13; Shutterstock Images, 15; Claude Paris/AP Images, 17; De Agostini Picture Library/Getty Images, 19, 20–21, 43; Hugh Rooney/Eye Ubiquitous/Universal Images Group/Getty Images, 23; Aliaksei Kruhlenia/Shutterstock Images, 25; Niglay Nik/Shutterstock Images, 28–29, 45; Science History Images/Alamy, 31; Oksana Perkins/Shutterstock Images, 33; Helen Hotson/Shutterstock Images, 35; Heritage Arts/Heritage Images/Hulton Archive/Getty Images, 37 (scraper); Sepia Times/Universal Images Group/Getty Images, 37 (Paleolithic hand axe); The Natural History Museum, London/Science Source, 37 (barbed point); Science & Society Picture Library/Getty Images, 37 (Mesolithic hand axe); C. M. Dixon/Print Collector/Hulton Archive/Getty Images, 37 (axe); G. Dagli Orti/DEA/De Agostini/Getty Images, 37 (harpoon); Lanmas/Alamy, 39; Sonia Bonet/Shutterstock Images, 40

Editor: Laura Stickney
Series Designer: Ryan Gale

Library of Congress Control Number: 2024938379

Publisher's Cataloging-in-Publication Data

Names: LaPierre, Yvette, author.
Title: The Stone Age / by Yvette LaPierre
Description: Minneapolis, Minnesota: ABDO Publishing, 2025 | Series: Historical ages | Includes online resources and index.
Identifiers: ISBN 9781098295660 (lib. bdg.) | ISBN 9798384916666 (ebook)
Subjects: LCSH: History, Ancient--Juvenile literature. | Stone age--Juvenile literature. | Hand tools--Juvenile literature. | Flintknapping--Juvenile literature. | Hunting and gathering societies—Juvenile literature. | Civilization and science--Juvenile literature. | History--Juvenile literature. | Historical archaeology--Juvenile literature. | Anthropology, Prehistoric--Juvenile literature.
Classification: DDC 930.11--dc23

CONTENTS

Zur Erinnerung
an die Entdeckung
DES
Neandertal-
Menschen
DURCH
Prof. Dr. C. Fuhlrott
ELBERFELD
im Sommer 1856
NEANDERTHAL FUNDSTELLE

CHAPTER ONE

STONE AGE DISCOVERY

One day in August 1856, workers were digging for limestone in the Neander Valley in Germany. As they worked, their shovels hit some bones. The bones were buried in a thick layer of clay inside a cave. As the workers shoveled, a skull emerged. They unearthed more bones. The workers thought the bones were from a bear, so they tossed them into a pile of other items from the cave. But the man in charge of

In Germany, a plaque marks the site of Kleine Feldhofer Grotte, the cave where Neanderthal bones were discovered in 1856. The cave no longer exists, but visitors can explore a museum near the site.

the dig rescued the bones. He set them aside for the local schoolteacher, Johann Carl Fuhlrott. Fuhlrott was interested in natural history.

Fuhlrott took the bones home to inspect them. Unlike a modern human skull, the skull from the cave had almost no chin. Its forehead angled back low over where the brain would be. The skull had a bulging ridge over the eyes. The back had a bulge at the base.

The other bones were big and thick. The thigh bones curved. Fuhlrott laid the bones out in the shape of a skeleton. Later, he took the bones to a professor of anatomy. Together, Fuhlrott and the

SKELETON SCIENTISTS

Many types of scientists work to understand Stone Age people. Anthropologists study skeletons and other human remains. They learn about human history and culture. Archaeologists study the objects that people left behind, such as tools, art, and buildings. These scientists are like detectives, using special tools and methods to dig in the ground and find clues about people from the past.

The Neanderthal bones discovered in 1856 included rib fragments, several arm and leg bones, and the top part of a skull.

professor concluded that the bones were the remains of an ancient human. Later, other researchers realized that several remains found prior to 1856 were the same type of ancient human. In 1864, this early species became known as Neanderthals. The species was named after the place where the first skeleton had been found. It was the first extinct human species to be named.

Researchers made a model of a Neanderthal man based on the bones discovered in Neander Valley. In 2009, a model of a Neanderthal woman was displayed next to the man.

WHAT WAS THE STONE AGE?

Archaeologists are historians who uncover human remains and artifacts from the past. They study these remains to determine what early humans looked like and where they lived. Artifacts buried with skeletons hold clues about what tools and items early humans used. From their studies, archaeologists know that Neanderthals were one of several human species that lived during the Stone Age.

The Stone Age began when early humans in Africa first made tools out of stone. The period ended when people in Mesopotamia, a region in what is now southwestern Asia, made tools out of bronze for the first time. This led to the Bronze Age. The Stone Age lasted from roughly 2.5 million years ago to 3300 BCE. The dates for the period are not exact. People in different parts of the world entered the Stone Age at different times. This is because they invented tools at different times.

Humans developed and changed in significant ways during the Stone Age. Early Stone Age people hunted for meat and gathered food.

STONE AGE HUMANS

All humans belong to a species family of upright-walking apes called hominins. Early in the Stone Age, the first hominins learned how to make stone tools. They moved from Africa to Europe and Asia, evolving into different species. Several human groups lived during the Stone Age. For example, Neanderthals and modern humans may have lived side by side for up to 8,000 years.

STAGES OF THE STONE AGE

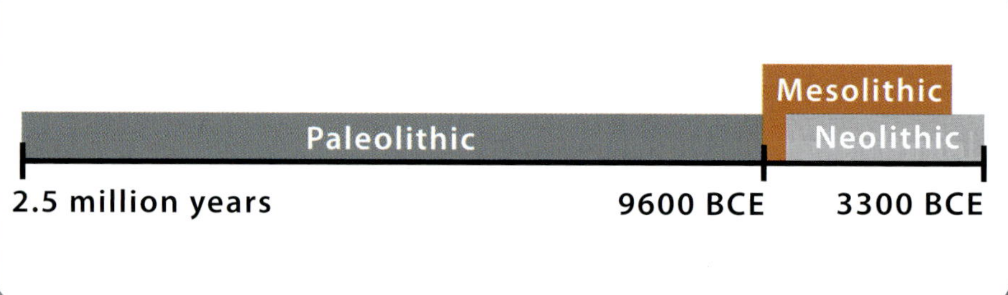

This timeline shows the approximate years of each stage of the Stone Age. These dates vary across different parts of the world. What do you notice about the length of each stage? Which stages are longer than others?

They lived in small groups. They were nomadic, moving with the seasons to find food. Caves and rock ledges served as their homes.

By the end of the Stone Age, people in many parts of the world had learned to farm. They planted crops and raised animals such as cattle, sheep, and pigs. Many people no longer needed to move in search of food. They built more permanent homes. Soon, small groups of houses and buildings grew into villages. The Stone Age is divided into three main periods. These are called the Paleolithic, the Mesolithic, and the Neolithic.

STRAIGHT TO THE SOURCE

Stephen E. Nash is a historian and archaeologist. He thinks most people have the wrong idea about what Stone Age people were like. He said:

> *When most members of the general public think of the Stone Age, they probably envision an adult male hominin wielding a stone tool. . . . Why do many people assume that only men worked with stone tools? This is simply because Western society holds dear a[n] . . . idea that men are hunters, women are gatherers, and the latter should tend to the home. Combine that with the fact that until recently, the vast majority of archaeologists have been men, and we end up with a situation in which women's work, and even more so, children's work and play, have not received proper scholarly attention. Women and children are often rendered invisible in reconstructions of past human societies.*

Source: Stephen E. Nash. "Stone Age Myths We've Made Up." *Sapiens*, 19 July 2019, sapiens.org. Accessed 4 Feb. 2024.

WHAT'S THE BIG IDEA?

Take a close look at this passage. What point is the author making about Stone Age people and how modern people think of them? What details does the author use to support this idea?

CHAPTER TWO

PALEOLITHIC

The Paleolithic is the earliest stage of the Stone Age. It is sometimes called the Old Stone Age. It began at least 2.5 million years ago, when people in Africa first made stone tools. This period overlapped with an Ice Age. During this time, much of the water on Earth was frozen. The Paleolithic was also the longest stage of the Stone Age. The period covered almost three million years of human history, ending in roughly 9600 BCE.

During the Paleolithic, early humans hunted large animals such as mammoths. They likely hunted in groups and used weapons such as spears.

EARLY TOOLMAKERS

Throughout the Paleolithic, early human species evolved and developed. Scientists group most toolmaking species into the *Homo* genus. Some of the first humans to make stone tools are now called *Homo habilis*, or "handy man." They lived across Africa. They made cutting tools out of chipped stone. Archaeologists have discovered *Homo habilis* remains and tools at sites such as Olduvai Gorge in Tanzania.

Other hominins that lived during the Stone Age included *Homo erectus*, *Homo neanderthalensis*, and *Homo sapiens*. *Homo erectus* lived between about 1.8 million years ago and 110,000 years ago. It was the first human species to walk completely upright. *Homo erectus* used fire and made stone hand axes and cleavers. *Homo neanderthalensis* evolved about 400,000 years ago. This species made more complex tools, such as stone scrapers and spears. They also buried their dead. *Homo sapiens*, or modern humans, appeared about 300,000 years ago. They had larger

A statue at Olduvai Gorge in Tanzania features two models of Paleolithic skulls found at the site. It includes a *Homo habilis* skull, *right,* and the skull of a species called *Paranthropus boisei, left.*

brains than other Stone Age humans. Neanderthals went extinct about 40,000 years ago. Modern humans were the last human species remaining for the rest of the Stone Age and beyond.

PALEOLITHIC LIFE

Paleolithic peoples likely lived in small groups. They used caves and overhanging rocks as shelter. They lived as hunter-gatherers, moving with the seasons to follow animals and find food. People fished, hunted animals, and gathered wild plants, fruits, nuts, and berries. They cooked their food over fires.

Paleolithic peoples were the first to make art, starting about 40,000 years ago. They made small sculptures out of clay, stone, and bone. They painted and carved designs on cave walls, too. They used red and black paint to leave prints of their hands on rock walls. The paint was made from minerals. Chauvet Cave in southern France is home to some of the best-preserved Paleolithic wall art. The images include handprints and hundreds of animals.

CAVE ART

In 1994, three friends discovered Chauvet Cave in southern France. They wandered through the cave's chambers in awe. The walls were covered with breathtaking portraits of animals. About 400 images of Ice Age animals, including mammoths, lions, wild horses, woolly rhinoceroses, and owls, were carved or painted onto the wall. The art was 36,000 years old. That was twice as old as cave art that had been discovered earlier.

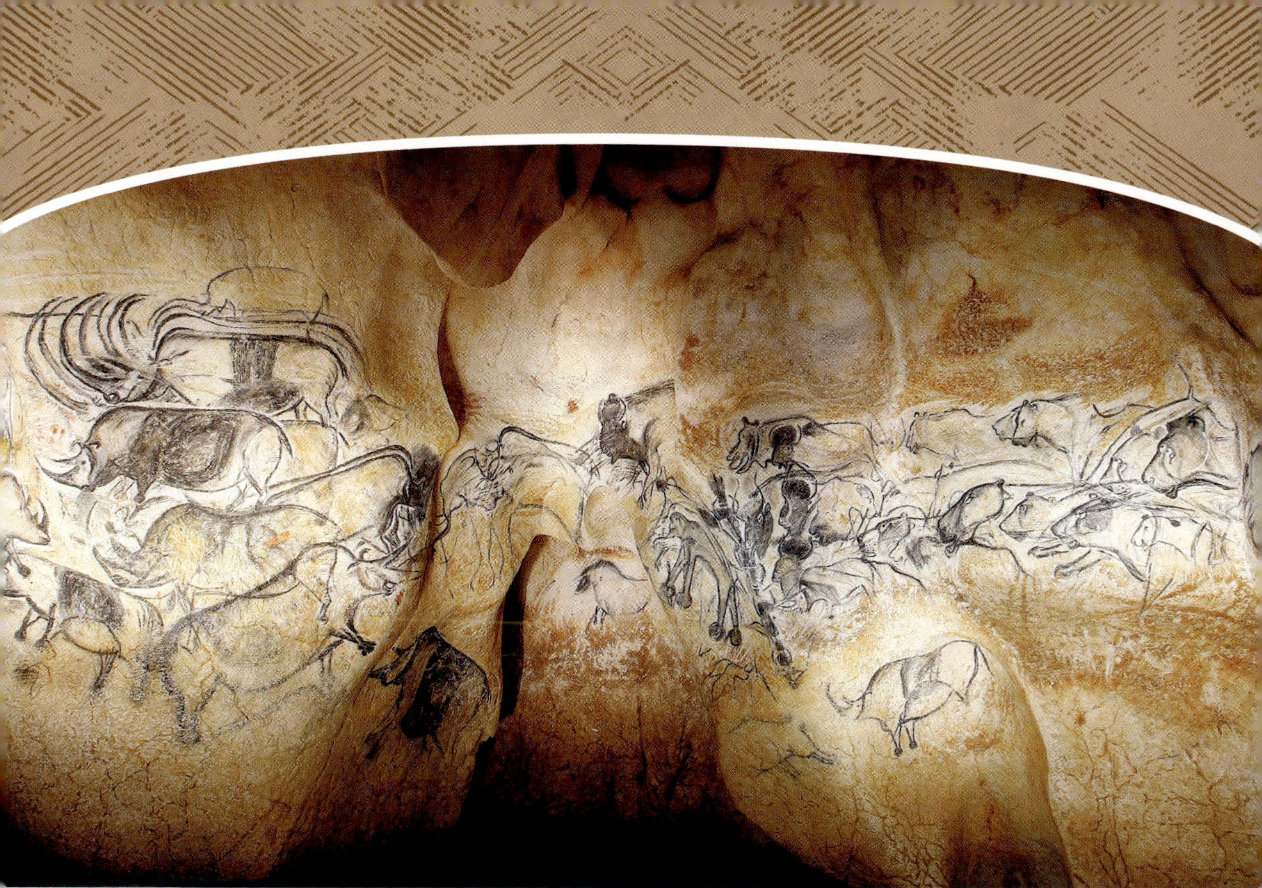

The Paleolithic art in Chauvet Cave features images of horses, lions, bison, rhinos, and more. Today, visitors can walk through a full-sized replica of the cave to see reproductions of the art.

PALEOLITHIC TOOLS

Paleolithic peoples made tools out of stones, which were strong and plentiful. The earliest tools were rocks that people struck with other stones to make jagged edges. This process is called knapping.

One example of an early tool is the hammerstone. This was a fist-sized tool with a sharpened edge.

STONE AGE ANIMALS

Some Stone Age animals were much larger than their modern relatives. Mammoths were land animals that were about the size of elephants. They had fur and curved tusks. Woolly mammoths adapted to withstand the bitter cold of the Ice Age. The dire wolf was about the size of a modern gray wolf. But it was heavier and had bigger teeth for hunting prey. The saber-toothed cat was likely shorter and heavier than a modern-day lion. It had long, sharp canine teeth that extended from its upper jaw. Many Stone Age animals went extinct due to hunting by early humans and the warming climate at the end of the Ice Age.

The sharp flakes people chipped off stones were also used as tools. Other Paleolithic tools were made of bone, wood, and ivory.

As the Paleolithic progressed, so did toolmaking techniques. People continued to shape rocks with stone and bone tools to make straighter, sharper edges. They created thinner tools such as hand axes, which had two sharpened edges.

People used stone tools for many tasks. These included

Paleolithic people made tools out of stones and animal bones. They may have used scraping tools to make animal skins into clothing.

hunting, cutting meat, and scraping animal skins. People also used stone tools to dig up plants, mash up roots, and break open nuts and bones.

EXPLORE ONLINE

Chapter Two discusses art in the early Stone Age. The website below explores Chauvet Cave, a site full of Paleolithic art. As you know, every source is different. How is the information from the website similar to the information in Chapter Two? What new information did you learn from the website?

MEET OUR ANCESTORS: CHAUVET CAVE

abdocorelibrary.com/stone-age

CHAPTER THREE

MESOLITHIC

The Mesolithic, also known as the Middle Stone Age, lasted from roughly 9600 BCE to 4000 BCE, depending on the region. During this time, the world's climate warmed. This changed the environment. Icy glaciers melted, which caused the seas to rise. As ice and snow retreated, forests grew. Lakes and rivers formed. The lifestyles and toolmaking techniques of Mesolithic peoples changed in response to the end of the Ice Age.

Archaeologists have found evidence that Mesolithic people used tools such as traps, hooks, and harpoons to catch fish.

MESOLITHIC LIFE

Mesolithic peoples continued to live in small groups as hunter-gatherers. Plants were able to grow better in the warmer climate, which meant that a greater variety of food was available. People gathered wild plants to eat. They hunted animals such as deer, bears, and rabbits for meat and skins. They also ate other animals, including fish, frogs, birds, and snails.

Mesolithic peoples continued to move around in search of food. But they became so skilled at hunting and gathering that they could stay in one place for longer

ICE AGES

Throughout the Stone Age, people lived through several Ice Ages. These are periods when freezing temperatures cause ice to cover large parts of the world. The last Ice Age lasted for thousands of years. It ended in about 10,000 BCE, at the beginning of the Mesolithic. Stone Age peoples survived and thrived in these cold times. They used animal skins and fur to make warm clothes and shelters. They spent time indoors creating art, passing on knowledge, and planning for the future.

At Irish National Heritage Park in Ireland, visitors can see a reconstructed Mesolithic camp. The camp shows what shelters might have looked like during the period.

periods of time. They began to spend full seasons living in settlements near bodies of water. These seasonal settlements later became the first permanent villages.

MESOLITHIC TOOLS

Mesolithic peoples made tools out of stone, bone, ivory, and antlers. Toolmakers made many stone tools out of flint. They struck long, straight flakes from big stones to create sharp blades. They used these blades to carve antler and bone into other tools. People also attached small blades to long antlers, bones, or pieces of wood. These served as spears and arrows. Larger tools included stone clubs, wooden bows and arrows, and stone axes with wooden handles. Many Mesolithic tools have been found at the Star Carr site in North Yorkshire, England. Archaeologists have discovered harpoons, axes, and more at the site.

Mesolithic peoples developed new tools to deal with their changing environment. One such tool was the adze. This cutting tool was used to carve wood into fishing platforms and dugout canoes. People used these for fishing in the rivers and lakes that had formed at the end of the Ice Age. People also used harpoons and fishing hooks. Another tool was a stone scraper. This was used to scrape flesh and hair from animal hides. Mesolithic peoples also made stone awls. These small, pointed tools punched holes in hides. These holes

At the Lepenski Vir archaeological site in Serbia, people can see the remains of a Mesolithic settlement.

allowed people to tie hides together to make clothes and shelters.

FIRST FARMERS

As the Mesolithic Period ended, people began farming. Farming started at different times in different parts of the world. As a result, there's no single date for the end of the Mesolithic. In fact, farming began so early in some parts of the world that some people went straight from the Paleolithic to the Neolithic Period.

EARLY HUMANS' BEST FRIEND

By about 15,000 years ago, Stone Age peoples had domesticated dogs. With their strong eyesight and sense of smell, dogs were excellent helpers during hunts. People likely used them to guard their homes and haul heavy items. Dogs were more than just useful, though. Researchers believe that Stone Age peoples treated dogs like pets. Archaeologists have found graves in which humans and dogs were buried together. In 1914, archaeologists discovered a 14,000-year-old puppy skeleton buried in a grave in Germany. Later studies showed that the dog was cared for through several illnesses. This suggests that Stone Age peoples cared deeply for their dogs, just as humans do today.

People in Egypt and southwestern Asia became the first farmers around 10,000 years ago. They planted, harvested, and stored crops. They also began raising and keeping animals for food and work. They settled into permanent villages near their fields. The arrival of farming ushered in a new era called the Neolithic. In some areas of the world, where people still lived as hunter-gatherers, the Mesolithic continued.

STRAIGHT TO THE SOURCE

Practical stone tools weren't the only thing that Stone Age peoples made. Archaeologists have found toys that Stone Age people crafted for their children. An article in *Smithsonian* magazine discussed these toys:

> *Archaeologists believe that children in the [Middle Paleolithic] played with . . . pointed sticks and thereby developed throwing and hunting skills. . . . The Upper Paleolithic version of flipbooks, rondelles are small disks made of bone, antler or ivory, with an image carved on either side and one or two holes for a cord in the middle. Tug the cord back and forth, and the disk swings, giving the illusion of a moving image. One [Ice Age] example found in France in 1868 shows a doe with her legs tucked under her on one side and extended on the other, so it looks like she is running when the rondelle is swinging.*

Source: Jaimie Seaton. "Home Games." *Smithsonian*, Dec. 2023, smithsonianmag.com. Accessed 28 May 2024.

BACK IT UP

The author of this passage is using evidence to support a point. Write a paragraph describing the point the author is making. Then write down two or three pieces of evidence the author uses to make the point.

CHAPTER FOUR

NEOLITHIC

During the Neolithic, or New Stone Age, people began to leave behind their hunter-gatherer lifestyles to become farmers. The Neolithic began at least 10,000 years ago in parts of the Middle East. It started later in other parts of the world. In southeastern Europe, the period likely began in 7000 BCE. East Asia entered the period in 6000 BCE. The Neolithic was a time of great advancement in technology and people's ways of life.

At the ancient city of Çatalhöyük in Turkey, archaeologists have found evidence that Neolithic people ate crops such as wheat, barley, and rye. They also raised animals such as sheep.

RISE OF FARMING

The first farmers worked in an area of the Middle East known as the Fertile Crescent. This crescent-shaped region spans what are now the countries of Iraq, Turkey, Syria, Lebanon, Israel, Palestine, and Egypt. People in the Fertile Crescent developed agriculture, or the practice of planting, harvesting, and storing crops. They planted various crops, including wheat, barley, and lentils. They grew nut and fruit trees. Neolithic farmers also raised animals,

THE LAST HUMANS LEFT

Neanderthals roamed Europe and western Asia for hundreds of thousands of years. They made stone tools, hunted, created art, cared for each other, and buried their dead. By about 40,000 years ago, their numbers dwindled as *Homo sapiens* spread and thrived. The Neanderthals' last known outpost was a cave in Gibraltar, located south of Spain. They disappeared from the fossil record about 28,000 years ago. The closest relatives of modern humans became extinct. Modern humans were the last human species left on Earth.

Neolithic people likely used tools such as hoes to farm crops.

including cattle, goats, and sheep. Evidence of early farming has been found at Tell Aswad in Syria, which was excavated between 2001 and 2007. At this farming settlement, archaeologists have discovered remains of wheat and barley.

Later, people in eastern Asia and Europe began farming too. The types of crops and animals that people raised depended on the region in which they lived. Farming gave Stone Age peoples a steady and abundant food supply for the first time. As a result, the lives of Neolithic peoples changed tremendously. With a steady food supply, Neolithic peoples did not need to move from place to place in search of food. This allowed them to settle in one place year-round. With more food available, more people could be fed. Because of this, Neolithic populations rose.

As populations increased, permanent settlements grew into villages. This was a big change from the small family bands of the past. More complex societies developed. For the first time, large groups of people lived together in an organized way. They learned how to make decisions as a group and share the work that needed to be done.

Skara Brae, located in Scotland's Orkney Islands, is one of the best-preserved Neolithic settlements in Western Europe. The site is home to several Neolithic homes.

5

ÇATALHÖYÜK

About 9,400 years ago, Neolithic people built Çatalhöyük, the earliest known city. It was located in what is now central Turkey. People in the area settled there to grow crops and herd animals. They built rows of mud-brick houses on top of each other. These houses had large openings in the roofs to let smoke out and let sunlight in. People moved around the city across the rooftops. All the houses were similar in size and construction. Because of this, experts believe Çatalhöyük was a society in which everyone was equal.

In addition to farming and herding, villagers had other work to do. They cut down trees and cleared land for crops and villages. They built houses and other structures. Depending on which part of the world they lived in, people built houses out of mud bricks, stone, or wood. The houses were usually small, one-room buildings clustered together. People piled mounds of earth to create enclosures, which protected homes and animals. In many places, people built large tombs of earth, wood, or stone to bury their dead. One example of a Neolithic

Some Neolithic people built stone structures known as dolmens. They were likely used as tombs or monuments.

settlement is Skara Brae in Scotland. This site features homes built out of stone slabs.

A CULTURED LIFE

A settled life and a steady supply of food gave Neolithic peoples more time for other activities. They created new art forms. People continued to create paintings and sculptures. They also engaged in drawing, pottery, and weaving. People developed trade routes for goods too. They invented new tools and techniques to turn stone, bone, wood, and ivory into decorative items, such as jewelry.

Forms of dancing and music developed. In some areas, people created elaborate masks to use in ceremonies. Shared activities, art, and rituals helped draw people together as a community.

FINER TOOLS

Neolithic peoples used a wide variety of tools. These included axes and adzes, which were used to clear forests and till the land. People also made polished chisels, gouges, and saws. They used these to turn wood into houses, furniture, and other useful items.

These tasks required more sophisticated tools. Neolithic peoples still made many stone tools by chipping them to create sharp edges. But they also spent more time finishing the rough edges of the tools. After chipping a stone tool into shape, the toolmaker rubbed its edges with a sharp rock to create a smoother edge. Then the toolmaker used a finer rock to polish the tool's edge. This made the tool sharper, straighter, and stronger.

STONE AGE TOOLS

Throughout the Stone Age, people developed new types of tools. This graphic shows examples of tools from the Paleolithic, Mesolithic, and Neolithic. How are these tools similar and different? Why do you think these tools changed over time?

PALEOLITHIC

Scraper

Hand axe

MESOLITHIC

Barbed point

Hand axe

NEOLITHIC

Axe

Harpoon

People also used small stone flakes to carve wood, antler, and bone into harpoon points and needles. They carved sculptures and other decorative items too. They even made musical instruments such as bone flutes.

TRADE

Neolithic peoples found many of the materials they used to make tools and art near their settlements. But other materials came from far away. Neolithic peoples found ways to trade shells, precious stones, amber, and more with others across long distances.

One example is a set of necklace beads found in the grave of a child buried 9,000 years ago in what is now Jordan. Researchers reconstructed the necklace. Its strands held more than 2,500 beads. The beads were made from a variety of materials, including turquoise, shells, amber, and reddish limestone.

Archaeologists have uncovered many pieces of Neolithic jewelry. Some Neolithic necklaces discovered in Spain have beads made of a mineral called variscite.

At Stonehenge, which is located on England's Salisbury Plain, visitors can see reconstructed Neolithic houses.

The limestone came from near the burial site. But the other materials came from far away. This suggests that Neolithic villages were connected to each other through a trade network.

END OF AN ERA

The Stone Age came to an end when people learned how to make tools out of metal. This happened at different times in different places around the world.

People in central Europe and western Asia made the first metal tools out of copper in around 5000 BCE.

In about 3500 BCE, people in western Asia began mixing tin with copper to create bronze, a much harder metal. Between 1600 BCE and 1700 BCE, people in China started this practice too. This marked the beginning of the Bronze Age. This period would usher in a new era of human development. But the stone tools perfected during the Stone Age continued to be used around the world for centuries to come.

FURTHER EVIDENCE

Chapter Four explores how toolmaking techniques changed throughout the Stone Age. What is the main point of this chapter? What key evidence supports this point? Go to the article about Stone Age tools at the website below. Find a quote from the website that supports this chapter's main point.

STONE TOOLS

abdocorelibrary.com/stone-age

IMPORTANT DATES

2.5 million years ago
Early people make stone tools for the first time. The Paleolithic Period begins.

40,000 years ago
Paleolithic people make art for the first time.

10,000 BCE–9600 BCE
The Ice Age ends, and the Mesolithic Period begins. The Neolithic Period begins. People in Egypt and southwestern Asia start farming.

5000 BCE
People in central Europe and western Asia make the first metal tools from copper. This marks the beginning of the Bronze Age.

4000 BCE
The Mesolithic Period ends.

3300 BCE
The Neolithic Period ends, marking the end of the Stone Age.

1856 CE
Workers discover Neanderthal remains while digging in the Neander Valley in Germany.

1994
Paleolithic art is discovered in Chauvet Cave in France.

2001–2007
Archaeologists excavate the Tell Aswad site in Syria.

STOP AND THINK

Tell the Tale

Chapter One of this book discusses how people discovered an ancient human skeleton while digging in the Neander Valley in Germany. Imagine you are making a similar discovery at a Stone Age burial site. Write 200 words about the artifacts you find. What do your discoveries tell you about the ancient people who lived at the site?

Surprise Me

This book discusses the lives of Stone Age people. After reading this book, what two or three facts about Stone Age life did you find most surprising? Write a few sentences about each fact. Why did you find each fact surprising?

Why Do I Care?

The Stone Age happened a long time ago, and Stone Age people lived very different lives from modern humans. But that doesn't mean you can't think about why the period was important. How did Stone Age inventions and tools affect how humans live? Does learning about the Stone Age help you better understand how people live today?

You Are There

Chapter Four describes Neolithic cities and settlements. Imagine you are visiting one of these cities thousands of years ago. Write a letter home telling your friends about what the city is like. Be sure to add plenty of detail to your notes.

GLOSSARY

anatomy
the study of the bodies and bones of animals or humans

domesticate
to tame, raise, and keep for human use or as a pet

evolve
to develop or change over time

excavate
to dig up the ground to uncover artifacts or remains

extinct
no longer living or existing

fertile
able to produce healthy plant growth

flint
a type of hard rock

genus
a scientific grouping of species that are related

harpoon
a type of spear used when hunting or fishing

nomadic
relating to people who move from place to place instead of living permanently in one place

species
a group of living things that share characteristics and can produce offspring with each other

ONLINE RESOURCES

To learn more about the Stone Age, visit our free resource websites below.

Visit **abdocorelibrary.com** or scan this QR code for free Common Core resources for teachers and students, including vetted activities, multimedia, and booklinks, for deeper subject comprehension.

Visit **abdobooklinks.com** or scan this QR code for free additional online weblinks for further learning. These links are routinely monitored and updated to provide the most current information available.

LEARN MORE

Everything: Stone Age to Iron Age. National Geographic Kids, 2021.

Walmsley, Naomi. *Live Like a Hunter Gatherer: Discovering the Secrets of the Stone Age*. Button Books, 2022.

INDEX

About the Author

Yvette LaPierre lives in North Dakota with her family and has written more than 30 books for young readers. She enjoys learning about early humans and hopes that she has a Neanderthal as an ancestor.